PowerKiDS
Readers
MY COMMUNITY

A TRIP TO THE
LIBRARY

Josie Keogh

PowerKiDS
press™

New York

Published in 2013 by The Rosen Publishing Group, Inc.
29 East 21st Street, New York, NY 10010

First Edition

Editor: Amelie von Zumbusch
Book Design: Ashley Drago

Photo Credits: Cover, pp. 5, 6, 9, 21 Shutterstock.com; p. 10 Sam Bloomberg-Rissman/Blend Images/Getty Images; p. 13 Livia Corona/Stone/Getty Images; p. 14 Ableimages/Riser/Getty Images; p. 17 © www.iStockphoto.com/Kyu Oh; p. 18 Andy Crawford/Dorling Kindersley/Getty Images; p. 22 © www.iStockphoto.com/kali9.

Library of Congress Cataloging-in-Publication Data

Keogh, Josie.
  A trip to the library / by Josie Keogh. — 1st ed.
    p. cm. — (Powerkids readers: my community)
  Includes index.
  ISBN 978-1-4488-7402-6 (library binding) — ISBN 978-1-4488-7481-1 (pbk.) —
  ISBN 978-1-4488-7555-9 (6-pack)
  1. Libraries—Juvenile literature. I. Title.
  Z665.5.K46 2013
  020—dc23
                          2011047407

Manufactured in the United States of America

CPSIA Compliance Information: Batch #CS12PK: For Further Information contact Rosen Publishing, New York, New York at 1-800-237-9932

CONTENTS

Mr. Lee's class went to the library.

5

It was fun!

7

Ms. Gray read to them.

10

The kids picked books.

Kim got a book on dogs.

13

Josh found one on cars.

Matt wanted a book on cats.
Ms. Gray found one.

Ms. Hall checked the books out.

19

The kids took the books home.

They will be due in two weeks.

23

WORDS TO KNOW

fiction: Stories.

librarian: A person who works in a library.

nonfiction: Books of facts.

INDEX

WEBSITES

Due to the changing nature of Internet links, PowerKids Press has developed an online list of websites related to the subject of this book. This site is updated regularly. Please use this link to access the list: www.powerkidslinks.com/pkrc/lib/